THE COMING
GLORY

HOPE NOW FOR
LIFE AFTER DEATH

*To my friend
—the lady with the
giving attitude
Bob*

Paul W. Swets

The Coming Glory: Hope Now for Life After Death
ISBN: 9781973406204

Imprint: TBA

Also by Paul W. Swets

The Art of Talking So That People Will Listen

(Simon & Schuster)

The Art of Talking With Your Teenager (Adams Media)

Dreaming Big (Authentic Publishing)

Finding Happiness (Crosslink Publishing)

Basketball Adventure (No Sweat Publishing)

For further information, go to the author's website
www.findinghappiness.info/the-coming-glory

CONTENTS

DEDICATION

The Coming Glory is dedicated to individuals and families who suffer the grief of impending death and want true hope.

I consider that the sufferings of this present time are not worth comparing with the glory that is to be revealed to us.
Romans 8:18

READER COMMENTS

"*The Coming Glory* is a gentle word for a difficult time. Paul offers an honest, truthful and hopeful journey for any facing the reality of death. It will honor your journey. It will awaken you to a future hard to imagine. It will prayerfully hold your hand as you walk through the valley. Frankly, I couldn't stop reading *The Coming Glory*. I was moved by the truth, I was moved by Paul's honesty, I was moved by his courage. I was moved to tears by this last paragraph: 'The time for my departure is getting closer day by day. Although I deeply love this life, I can hardly wait for the coming glory.'"

- **Rev. Jon Brown**, Senior Pastor at Pillar Church

"GLORIOUS!! I have just finished reading *The Coming Glory* and I have tears in my eyes, thinking of the people who will be comforted and encouraged through the last stage of their earthly journey, and their loved ones too. So much to love about this book—it is saturated in scripture, Paul's pastor's heart shines through every word, it is theologically rich, and the whole gospel is here. The way the author weaves in the great hymns and confessions of the faith is beautiful."

- **Rev. Dr. Suzanne McDonald**, Professor of Systematic and Historical Theology

"When I was a pastor, I would have been delighted to have these concise, well-crafted treatments of key eschatological themes. I would have valued especially a book like this to put in the hands of lay people facing death, along with their caring families. We meet a warm pastoral tone throughout the book. Readers will sense that they are hearing from a man with long experience and a caring heart."

- **Rev. Dr. William C. Brownson**, President Emeritus, Words of Hope

"So encouraging! I couldn't put it down. *The Coming Glory* would be a wonderful book for a small group book study. I like the large print. I was comforted by the appropriately placed Scripture and hymns. Paul has offered answers to seekers and those looking toward eternity."

- **Marty Greendonner**

"Tremendously inspiring! *The Coming Glory* is full of words that speak to the mind, heart, and soul with confidence and assurance as we face death. It would be an immensely helpful tool for ministers to give to parishioners facing life-and-death situations."

- **Rev. Dr. John W. Tien**, retired pastor

"The Rev. Dr. Paul Swets' book, *The Coming Glory,* is an inspiring read. His use of Scripture and his personal experiences enrich the book as he unfolds what the Bible teaches on the new heaven and new earth."

- **Bob DeYoung**

"*The Coming Glory* beautifully presents the end of our earthly lives in terms of a natural departure, leaving one place to go to another. Through an instructive lineup of Bible verses, Paul Swets shows how to find comfort for the journey and how you can know for certain that the astounding good news of heaven is for you!"

Carla Sinnema

"Helpful for someone facing death and for those looking for assurance and hope after having lost a loved one. I like the author's point about mystery because so much of what Christians believe has that overtone, but it brings us to the hope of glory.

- **Rev. Jim Neevel**, retired pastor

A NOTE to the READER

Death is not the end of our story. Glory is coming!

Life would be senseless, absurd, tragic if death were the final chapter of our story. Of course, it is no good to concoct an imagined future in order to feel better. We need truth—truth that draws us closer to the Author of our faith and prepares us for the coming glory.

Professor J. Todd Billings, who is wrestling with incurable cancer, writes, "For true hope in the face of death, we have nowhere else to go besides the Word of God, which finds its fulfillment in Jesus Christ."[1]

The Coming Glory will help you catch a glimpse of what the Word of God teaches about life after death. The Bible gives us an astounding perspective of God's glory, but does not tell us everything. Scripture reveals that the coming glory is the presence and power of God manifested in Christ and all his redeeming work. Our appropriate response is wonder, awe, and worship.

Mystery is abundant. The Apostle Paul acknowledges that mystery. As he considers the fact of the resurrection of Jesus Christ and the hope this gives to you and me, he exclaims,

> *No eye has seen, nor ear heard,*
> *nor the heart of mankind imagined,*
> *what God has prepared*
> *for those who love him.*
> 1 Corinthians 2:9-10

Like many Christians, you might be confused about the mystery of what is ahead. Yet, the Bible does reveal a true future reality glorious beyond compare.

Death is a present reality that stirs fearful emotions now. You likely have a bundle of feelings that must not be stifled. Please share your story and questions with a friend or pastor—someone who will hear you out and listen to your soul. Most importantly, pour out your anguish to the Wonderful

Counselor who loves you and knows you better than you know yourself.

As a minister of pastoral care, I have had the privilege of hearing the stories of hundreds of individuals and families in the midst of life-and-death crisis. What is needed then? A genuine friend. You might think of this little book as a friend that comes alongside you and gives you hope.

Endnotes at the back of the book provide information on source materials and biblical content not included in the text. Also, there is a recommended reading list and chapter summaries that give brief answers to each chapter question.

Dear friend, God's gospel can move us from anxious despair into calm assurance and true hope. My prayer is that the Holy Spirit will excite our minds and comfort our hearts with the plain (but mysterious) and simple (but profound) truth of the gospel.

Paul W. Swets
Holland, Michigan

Oh, the depth of the riches and wisdom and knowledge of God! How unsearchable are his judgments and how inscrutable his ways! For from him and through him and to him are all things. To him be glory forever! Amen.

Romans 11:33, 36

CHAPTER ONE

How Can I Prepare for My Departure?

The time for my departure has come.
Apostle Paul
2 Timothy 4:6

Departure is a gentle way of saying the Apostle Paul knows he's about to die.

You or a family member may be at the point of "departure." It is hard to accept this reality. We don't want to depart from all we know. We fear suffering—our own and that of our loved ones. We don't want to leave loved ones. We don't know what's on "the other side." We grieve deeply. Our sorrow, fear, and confusion are understandable.

In the midst of his suffering and grief, the Psalmist pleads with the Lord in this prayer of lament.

Be merciful to me, LORD, for
I am in distress;
my eyes grow weak with sorrow,
my soul and body with grief.
My life is consumed by anguish
and my years by groaning;
my strength fails because of my affliction,
and my bones grow weak.
Psalm 31:9-10

Thankfully, God hears our cries of lament; our passionate expressions of grief, even anger.

The Lord has heard my plea;
the Lord accepts my prayer.
Psalm 6:9

The LORD hears us! And he will answer according to what is best for us, but not always the way we want him to. God is God and we are not.

Mike prayed for relief, but he was dying. He knew it; his family knew it. He was firm in his faith. The family thought he was well prepared for death, but near the time for his departure, he said, "I'm confused." For the first time, he was face to face with an enormous new reality—his impending death. Uncertainty made him very uncomfortable.

Mike is like many facing their last days. I have had the privilege of coming alongside hundreds of them and their families—waiting, listening, comforting. I remember the intense emotions in the midst of grief: fear and confusion, yet sometimes magnificent peace and calm.

How do you or I prepare for death? After a heart attack, a five bypass surgery, a TAVR surgery, and an on-going Inclusion Body Myositis condition, I ponder this sobering question. It motivates me to prepare for my own departure.

"Departure" is the word Paul chooses—not dissolution, not destruction, not annihilation. *Departure* suggests leaving one place in order to go to another place, like a ship departing from one port to go to another port. Some have likened the death of a believer to leaving earth's shore, ideally with supportive family and friends gathered around, and arriving at heaven's shore to the cheers of the waiting heavenly host.

You or your loved ones might be facing a departure now. Questions abound not only about procedural details, but also *what happens to you after you leave earth's shore.* What you have believed all your life might not be clear or comforting. Perhaps you, like most of us, have *not* thought about the spiritual implications of death for yourself or your family…until now. Now is the best time to make sense of your condition at the end of this life. You can choose now to learn and believe the hope Scripture teaches.

Learn from the Apostle Paul. Paul knew he would die soon. He accepts it. In fact, he even looks forward to it. Why? He is convinced that:

For me to live is Christ,
and to die is gain.
Philippians 1:21

In his letter to Timothy, Paul mentions three actions that prepared him to depart in peace.

I have fought the good fight,
I have finished the race,
I have kept the faith.
2 Timothy 4:7

You and I might think we cannot say this with the confidence of Paul. After all, he was an Apostle. But even Paul admits times of inconsistency.

I do not understand my own actions.
For I do not do what I want, but
I do the very thing I hate.
Romans 7:15

Even though Paul regularly failed to live up to all his intentions, he is able to affirm three major facts about his life.

"I have fought the good fight"

Paul draws this image from his love of sports. In several other places, he uses metaphors from the Olympic games: fighting, running, training, and winning.

Notice, Paul says "I have fought the good *fight*..." Life *is* a battleground. Death *is* an enemy. Paul understands our struggle for faith, especially critical when death looms and when suffering, doubt, or temptation overwhelm. To Timothy and every believer, Paul encourages the fight against unbelief.

Fight the good fight of the faith.
Take hold of the eternal life
to which you were called...
1 Timothy 6:12

If you have been hurt in this fight, or feel you have already lost the battle for faith, do not despair. Victory is still possible. Even in the midst of doubt, call upon Jesus for help. Remember the father who came to Jesus and said,

I believe. Help my unbelief.
Mark 9:24

When you ask Jesus to help you believe him, Jesus will indeed help you. Then the amazing truth of the gospel will apply to you:

Death is swallowed up in victory.
1 Corinthians 15:54

Paul is saying that your death is not the end of the story. Christ's resurrection guarantees your victory. It's like the D-Day of World War II. Because the decisive battle had been won, victory was assured. Christ's resurrection is the decisive victory over death and it's a preview of the coming glory.

The strife is o'er, the battle done;
The victory of life is won;
The song of triumph has begun.
Alleluia!

"I have finished the race."

Think about the times you worked long and hard on a project and then experienced the joy of finishing it. Finish-line-joy related to completing one's life task was brought home to me in a shocking way. My family had gathered around my father's hospital bed as he was getting ready for his departure. Suddenly, with unusual strength, he sat up in bed, clapped his hands, and with a look of triumph said, "I'm dying!"

Did my father somehow hear "the distant triumph song?"

And when the strife is fierce,
the warfare long, steals on the ear
the distant triumph song, and hearts
are brave again, and arms are strong.
Alleluia, alleluia![2]

"I have kept the faith."

What does it mean to *keep* the faith? It means to commit to, to persevere, to maintain faith in Jesus even when the fight is hard and the failures many. It means to keep on believing in Jesus in spite of our botches.

For God so loved the world that
he gave his only son,
that whoever believes in him should not perish,
but have eternal life.
John 3:16

If you confess with your mouth that

Jesus is Lord
and believe in your heart that
God raised him from the dead,
you will be saved.
Romans 10:9

Does the Bible imply that all we need to do is just *say* the words and all will be well? No! What we confess with our mouth needs to come from the heart, the very core of our being. When our confession of faith is authentic, we will aim to believe and act in a way that fits a follower of Christ.

And by this we know that we have
come to know (Jesus), if we keep his
commandments.
1 John 2:3

Jesus summarized the commandments of God:

You shall love the Lord your God
with all your heart and with all your soul
and with all your mind.
This is the great and first commandment.
And a second is like it:
You shall love your neighbor as yourself.

Matthew 22:35-39

None of us have believed or kept God's commandments perfectly. But we can take heart because Jesus paid the penalty for sin through his death on the cross and offers forgiveness to all who trust in him.

God demonstrates his own love for us in this:
While we were still sinners,
Christ died for us.
Romans 5:8

There is therefore now no condemnation
for those who are in Christ Jesus.
Romans 8:1

It's never too late to ask Jesus to help you trust him, to declare with heart and mind as the early Christians did: "Jesus is my Lord!" This heartfelt affirmation enables you to experience the refreshment of God's complete forgiveness of your sin.

Repent, then, and turn to God, so that your
sins may be wiped out, that times of refreshing
may come from the Lord....
Acts 3:19

****

Summary

You can prepare for your departure by affirming your belief in Jesus Christ, who loves you and gives you eternal life.

Prayer

God, it's hard to get through my head that while I am yet a sinner, you still love me and want to save me.

I confess that I have not followed your commandments perfectly. I am sorry.
Please forgive my sins.

Thank you for your love shown to me in Jesus. Please give me faith that Christ is the one who will save me, just as I am, and give me hope now for life after death.
Amen.

Into your hand I commit my spirit;
You have redeemed me,
O LORD, faithful God.

I trust in you, O LORD;
I say, "You are my God."
My times are in your hand.
Psalm 31:5,15

CHAPTER TWO

What Happens Right After Death?

We would rather be away from the body and at home with the Lord.
2 Corinthians 5:8

Home! What does "home" mean to you? At best, the idea of our earthly home includes:
- Family that brings out the best in each other
- Feeling safe in an atmosphere of love
- A place where I don't have to hide who I am.

After death, we have a home that will surpass the best this life can offer because we will be "at home with the Lord."

When the Apostle Paul says he would rather be "away from the body and at home with the Lord," he is referring to heaven or paradise, the intermediate state between a Christian's death and the resurrection of the body. When we die, our physical bodies will be left behind here on earth, but our souls (our unique personality that make us different from every other person) will go immediately into the presence of Christ. Jesus said to the thief on the cross,

> *Truly I tell you, today*
> *you will be with me in paradise.*
> Luke 23:43

"Paradise" refers to a state of restful happiness in the presence of the Lord Jesus. Theologian N. T. Wright explains the meaning of paradise: "This state is not, clearly, the final destiny for which the Christian dead are bound, which is the bodily resurrection. But it is a state in which the dead are held firmly within the conscious love of God and the conscious presence of Jesus Christ while they await that day."[1]

The Bible does not tell us a great deal about this intermediate state. Lack of detail is part of the grand mystery of God. But Paul affirms what we do know happens when believers die: they enter a state of being "at home with the Lord"—*a joyful awareness of being with Jesus*—which Paul exclaims is "far better."

"Far better?" You and I might find it hard to agree that we would rather be "away from the body." Most of us have a built-in, God-given, desire to live as long as we can, unless suffering or despair overwhelm us in the present.

Yet Paul asserts it is *far better* to be away from the body because our souls will be "at home with the Lord." That means departure from the body at death is not a journey into nothingness or unconsciousness or sleep. Rather, it is a journey of the believer's soul into the very presence of Christ. The soul will be *with Christ*. We will be with the one who gave his very life to rescue us *from* a hellish state *for* triumphant glory!

Does our suffering now lessen the glory of being at home with the Lord? No, not according to the Apostle Paul.

For I consider that the sufferings
of this present time are not worth comparing
with the glory that is to be revealed to us.
Romans 8:18

Compared to the coming glory, any suffering we go through now will fade into insignificance. Why? Our suffering now can be swallowed up in *hope*—the eager anticipation of all God's promises fulfilled for every follower of Christ.

All God's promises are not completely fulfilled at death. We must still await the promise of the resurrection of our bodies. But immediately after we die, going home to be with the Lord will be glory unveiled for every believer.

Going home, going home,
I'm just going home.
Quiet-like, slip away -
I'll be going home.
It's not far, just close by;

Jesus is the Door;
Work all done, laid aside,
Fear and grief no more.
Friends are there, waiting now.
He is waiting, too.
See His smile! See His hand!
He will lead me through.[2]

****

Summary

Right after death, the soul (the true identity) of the believer is "at home with the Lord" and that is better than we can imagine.

Prayer

"Precious Lord, take my hand, lead me on, help me stand; I am tired, I am weak, I am worn; through the storm, through the night, lead me on to the light; take my hand, precious Lord, lead me home."[3]

Why are you cast down, O my soul,
and why are you in turmoil within me?
Hope in God; for I shall again praise him,
my salvation and my God.
Psalm 42:5

CHAPTER THREE

How Can I Get Ready for the Return of Christ?

*You must be ready, for the Son of Man is
coming at an hour you do not expect.*
Matthew 24:44

Our history is moving toward a tremendous
climax—*the return of Christ to this earth!*

Christ's return is a key teaching of the
New Testament:

*I will come again and take you to
myself, that where I am, you may be also.*
John 14:3

*This Jesus, who was taken up from you into
heaven, will come in the same way
as you saw him go into heaven.*
Acts 1:11

Mindful of our limited understanding of
the coming glory when Jesus appears, consider

the amazing events that Scripture indicates will occur:

- Dead bodies will be resurrected[1]
- The world as we know it will end and be transformed into a new creation[2]
- Christ will reign as Lord[3]
- The final judgement will occur[4]
- Unbelievers will be judged in their sins[5]
- Believers will be welcomed in their faith[6]
- Believers will experience heaven on the new earth.[7]

At one time scientists thought the earth was eternal; that it always existed. Since that time, scientists have discovered facts similar to what the Bible teaches; there was a beginning[8] and there will be an end.[9] Scripture teaches that the end of history, as we know it now, will happen when Christ returns to usher in the "new heavens and new earth"[10] (See Chapter Six).

If the return of Christ to earth staggers your imagination, good! You're on the right track. Nothing in our personal experience will compare to Christ's return.

Like the miracle of the "Incarnation"—*God taking on human flesh in Jesus Christ*—Christ's return will be a miracle of gigantic proportion. If it were not for the almighty power of God, who *created the universe*, the return of Christ would seem more like a wish than a future reality.

So what does the promised return of Jesus as reigning King mean to you and me? Since we all will experience this event,[11] why is the return of Christ important to think about now, even in the midst of distress?

The answer is that anticipating Christ's appearing motivates us to *prepare* now for his return, to experience the joyful *hope* the promise of his return provides, and to *wait* with courage and perseverance for the fulfillment of all God's promises in Christ.

Prepare

Jesus taught four parables about being ready for his return.[12] One of the stories is about ten virgins anticipating attending a wedding.[13] Five wise virgins had adequate oil for their lamps and were welcomed into the wedding feast. Five virgins were foolish because they had not made preparation. They were not allowed into the wedding feast. The point of the story is to plan ahead and be ready for the coming of the Bridegroom, i.e., the return of Christ.

You might be like the wise virgins who were prepared. You have prepared yourself by receiving Christ into your heart by faith. Or you might be like the foolish virgins who were not ready, who thought they would have plenty of time later to prepare. Christ taught that because you do not know when the Son of Man (Jesus) will come, prepare now, believe now, get your life in order now for eternity.

I tell you, now is the time of God's favor,
now is the day of salvation.
2 Corinthians 6:2

Hope

When you receive Christ's offer of salvation through faith in him, you can have hope—a rock solid confidence that Jesus will return and has prepared a place for you.

Let not your heart be troubled.
Believe in God; believe also in me.
In my Father's house are many rooms.
If it were not so, would I have told you
that I go to prepare a place for you?
And if I go and prepare a place for you,
I will come again and take you to myself,
that where I am, you may be also.
John 14:1-3

Oh, what comfort! As a believer, you have a place prepared by Christ! Our hope of a place at home with the Lord in the new creation is fulfilled when Christ returns. It provides inner peace now, even in the midst of turmoil.

Let us hold fast the confession
of our hope without wavering,
for he who promised is faithful.
Hebrews 10:23

We tend to be quickly troubled by many things—real, serious, immediate things—that can rob us of deep peace. Even so, Jesus made it clear that peace is available to us in spite of our troubles.

I have said these things to you,
that in me you may have peace.
In the world you will have tribulation.
But take heart. I have overcome the world.
John 16:33

Peace is based on the certain hope we have in Christ now—hope because Christ has promised those who believe in him will be saved. This hope motivates us to affirm: "Christ has died. Christ is risen. Christ will come again."[14] This is our hope now for eternity.

Wait

The New Testament stresses the certainty of Christ's return. For example, the last book of the Bible concludes with this promise of Jesus:

Surely, I am coming soon.

Revelation 22:20

Soon? Perhaps you are asking, "Why then must we wait? Why is the return of Christ so long in coming?" You and I are not alone in asking "Why the wait?" Even shortly after the resurrection of Christ, the Apostle Peter records that some were asking:

Where is this 'coming' he promised?
Ever since our fathers died, everything goes on
as it has since the beginning of creation.
2 Peter 3:4

Peter explains God's purpose for the delay:

Do not overlook this one fact, beloved,
that with the Lord one day is as a thousand
years, and a thousand years as one day.
The Lord is not slow to fulfill his promise
as some count slowness,
but is patient toward you,
not wishing that any should perish,
but that all should reach repentance.
2 Peter 3:8-9

Did you get it? The reason for the wait is God's mercy and love for you and all the world. He wants us all to repent and receive his gracious call to believe in Jesus.

Christ, having been offered once to bear the sins of many, will appear a second time, not to deal with sin, but to save those who are eagerly waiting for him.
Hebrews 9:28

Wendell Kimbrough relates in song the emotions of waiting and hoping:

Now the days and hours and moments of suffering seem so long, and the toil-some wait and wondering threaten silence to our song. Now our pain is real and pressing where our faith is thin and weak, but our hope is set on Jesus and we cling to him, our strength.[15]

****

Summary

When we set our hope on Jesus, who is our strength and who comforts us in our weakness, we will be ready for the return of Christ.

Prayer

Almighty God—Father, Son, and Holy Spirit —I praise you that in your great mercy you give all believers new birth into a living hope through the resurrection of Jesus Christ from the dead. I rejoice in the hope of the future return of Christ and an inheritance that can never perish, spoil or fade. Please help me in my suffering and grief. May my faith prove genuine and result in praise, glory and honor now and when Jesus Christ comes again. Come Lord Jesus. Amen.

(A prayer based on 1 Peter 1:3-9)

Be still before the LORD
and wait patiently for him ....
Psalm 37:7

CHAPTER FOUR

What Will Our Bodily Resurrection Be Like?

Behold, I tell you a mystery.
We shall not all sleep, but we all shall
be changed in a moment, in the twinkling
of an eye, at the last trumpet.
For the trumpet will sound,
and the dead will be raised imperishable,
and we shall be changed.
1 Corinthians 15:51-52

"The dead will be raised!" "We shall be changed!" At death *we rest in peace* (at home with the Lord), but at the return of Christ *we shall rise in glory*. Mystery indeed!

Scripture provides only faint indications of what the resurrection of our bodies will be like. And that may be all our finite minds can handle.

In this chapter we look at the glimpses we do have in Scripture about what the future holds—a coming glory beyond compare.

We know that when he (Jesus) appears
we shall be like him, because
we shall see him as he is.
1 John 3:2

The resurrection of Christ assures us of our own bodily resurrection. We shall be like him!

Our Historical Foundation

Historical fact lays the groundwork for our hope. We are not talking about wish fulfillment or mystic vision or conjecture. God's power raised Jesus Christ from the dead. This is the historical basis for the hope of our own bodily resurrection.

Even before the event of the resurrection, Jesus promised his disciples he would be raised.

*From that time Jesus began to show his
disciples that he must go to Jerusalem and
suffer many things..., and be killed,
and on the third day be raised.*
Matthew 16:21

Jesus does not merely say that he will be
raised (which is true), but something much
stronger. To Martha at the death of Lazarus,
Jesus declared:

*I am the resurrection and the life.
Whoever believes in me,
though he die, yet shall he live.*
John 11:25

Shortly after this conversation with
Martha, Jesus died on the cross to pay the
penalty for our sin. He was buried, and then
God raised him to life—a resurrection event
that changed history and undergirds the
Christian faith. Matthew records what
happened.

*On the first day of the week, at early dawn,
they went to the tomb, taking the spices they
had prepared. And they found the stone*

*rolled away from the tomb, but when they went
in they did not find the body of the Lord Jesus.
While they were perplexed about this,
behold, two men stood by them in dazzling
apparel. And as they were frightened and
bowed their faces to the ground,
the men said to them, "Why do you seek the
living among the dead? He is not here, but has
risen. Remember how he told you, while
he was still in Galilee, that the Son of Man
must be delivered into the hands of sinful men
and be crucified and on the third day rise.*
Luke 24:1-7

Paul the apostle recounts the historical
appearances of Christ after his resurrection.

*For I delivered to you as of first importance
what I also received: that Christ died for our
sins in accordance with the Scriptures,
that he was buried, that he was raised on the
third day..., and that he appeared to Cephas,
then to the twelve. Then he appeared to more
than five hundred brothers at one time,...
Then he appeared to James, then to all the
apostles. Last of all, as to one untimely born,
he appeared also to me.*
1 Corinthians 15:3-8

It is because of the historical fact of the resurrection of Christ that we have hope for our own resurrection. Death is not the end of our story, but the beginning of a new heavenly existence. Referring to this hope, the Apostle Peter praises God for Jesus' resurrection and what it means for us.

Blessed be the God and Father of our Lord Jesus Christ! According to his great mercy, he has caused us to be born again to a living hope through the resurrection of Jesus Christ from the dead....
1 Peter 1:3

Peter mentions "living hope" because Jesus' resurrection guarantees to us now that our bodies will be resurrected. Especially now, in the midst of suffering, our individual resurrection gives us hope. We can view our future as dynamic, exciting, awe-inspiring.

A Helpful Analogy

It would be foolish to think we can comprehend everything about our resurrected body. Yet, the Apostle Paul helps us understand what we can know by comparing our earthly bodies to a seed.

What you sow does not come to life unless it dies. And what you sow is not the body that is to be, but a bare kernel, perhaps of wheat or of some other grain. But God gives it a body as he has chosen, and to each kind of seed its own body. For not all flesh is the same, but there is one kind for humans, another for animals, another for birds, and another for fish. There are heavenly bodies and earthly bodies, but the glory of the heavenly is of one kind, and the glory of the earthly is of another.
1 Corinthians 15:36-40

Paul's analogy suggests there will be a *continuity* between our present selves and our resurrected selves—it's the same "seed." But there will be also a vast *difference*—now our bodies are "a bare kernel" compared to the fully developed resurrected body.

A Clear Comparison

Paul expands the description of our resurrected body with four contrasts.

1. Perishable vs. Imperishable

What is sown is perishable;
what is raised is imperishable.
1 Corinthians 15:42

Our present bodies are perishable; the seeds of death and disease are in them so that it's only a matter of time before they die. But we shall be raised imperishable. No more disease. No more pain. No more tears. No more danger. No more death.[1]

2. Dishonor vs Glory

It is sown in dishonor;
it is raised in glory.
1 Corinthians 15:43

Our bodies now are not perfect. We all have some defects that afflict the body, including sin. But our resurrected body will be glorious—not just on the outside, but also a glory from inside the transformed person. Philippians 3:21 says that the resurrected body will be like the glorified body of Christ—a real physical body that reflects the glory of God.

Can you imagine what your body will be like minus all imperfection? Theologian Anthony Hoekema says, "We shall not really know what this glory is like until we ourselves shall see it and experience it."[2]

3. Weakness vs Power

It is sown in weakness;
it is raised in power.
1 Corinthians 15:43

If you are like me, you get tired. You can't accomplish all you would like to do. You are always conscious of your limitations. As death approaches, we become totally weak, helpless. But at the time of the resurrection, this weak body will be raised in power. Can you imagine what your body "raised in power" will be like?

4. Natural vs Spiritual

It is sown a natural body;
it is raised a spiritual body.
1 Corinthians 15:44

A *spiritual body* is not the opposite of a *physical body*. Christ's resurrected body was definitely a physical one—he could be touched (John 20:17,27); he could eat food (Luke 24:38-43). But Christ's resurrected body was more than physical; it was also spiritual, a transformed physicality. *Our resurrected body will be more than physical, but not less than physical.* In other words, our resurrected body will be like Christ's resurrected body.

Our citizenship is in heaven, and from it we await a Savior, the Lord Jesus Christ, who will transform our lowly body to be like his glorious body, by the power that enables him even to subject all things to himself.
Philippians 3:20-21

Anthony Hoekema explains the viewpoint of Scripture: "Matter is not evil; it is part of God's good creation. Therefore the goal of God's redemption is the resurrection of the physical body, and the creation of a new earth on which his redeemed people can live and serve God forever with glorified bodies."[3]

In the midst of suffering, Paul assures us of God's plan for us in our future.

He who raised Christ from the dead will give life to your mortal bodies.
Romans 8:11

We ourselves… wait eagerly for… the redemption of our bodies.
Romans 8:23

What do these verses mean for you and me? Scripture teaches us there will be a change from our natural, weak, perishable body to a transformed resurrected body. When that happens, we will experience on the new earth the full blessings God provides.

Will we recognize family and friends in their resurrection bodies? That is our heart-warming hope. The disciples recognized Jesus in his resurrected body.

Although the Bible tells us very little about the exact nature of the resurrected body, we do know that when our resurrected bodies are like Christ's glorious body (Philippians 3:20-21), they will not be subject to decay and death. At the return of Christ, our bodies will be more wonderful than our grandest hopes.

****

Summary

The Bible describes our resurrected bodies as imperishable, glorious, powerful, spiritual bodies. This gives us hope now knowing that God will give us the final victory over every consequence of sin.

Prayer

O God, our help in the past and our hope for the future, open our eyes to your truth so that we may know you better, see our future more clearly, and face even suffering and death now with calm assurance, knowing that our bodies will be resurrected through Jesus Christ, our risen Lord. Amen.

I was brutish and ignorant;
I was like a beast toward you.
Nevertheless, I am continually with you.
You hold my right hand.
You guide me with your counsel,
and afterward you will receive
me to glory.
Psalm 73:22-24

CHAPTER FIVE

How Can I Face God's Judgment?

When justice is done,
it is a joy to the righteous
but terror to evildoers.
Proverbs 21:15

Since none of us have lived perfect lives, we may wonder how we will survive the judgment of God. Will God's judgment be a source of joy or terror for us?

In this chapter, we look at Scripture passages that remind us who God is and his gracious offer to us to escape the judgment our sin deserves.

Remember Who God Is

When the course of our lives does not go according to our plan, sometimes we wonder if God is judging us. Professor Todd Billings is considered by all who know him to be a very good person—but he suffers from incurable cancer. It's normal to ask, "Why?"

Perhaps you ask, "Why?" Why must I or my loved ones suffer? Why do bad things happen to good people? Todd's condition motivated a vigorous search in Scripture for guidance. He found an answer in the book of Job.

Job also was considered a good man, but some terrible things happened to his family and to him physically. In the midst of intense suffering, he yet gave clear testimony to his friends of his confidence in the future justice of God:

I know that my Redeemer lives,
and at the last he will stand upon the earth.
And after my skin has been thus destroyed,
yet in my flesh I shall see God,
whom I shall see for myself...
My heart faints within me!
Job 19:25-27

Even with Job's overwhelming confidence that he would "see God" after death, Job *laments* his present condition. He is in anguish because his suffering does not seem to be just. Something is not right. The opinions of his friends are not much help. He presents his case to God.

The Creator of the universe counsels Job to be mentally tough and to reflect on the vast difference between his limited understanding and the infinite wisdom of God.

> *Who is this that darkens counsel*
> *by words without knowledge?...*
> *Where were you when I laid*
> *the foundation of the earth?*
> *Tell me, if you have understanding.*
> Job 38:2,4

Todd Billings comments, "In the end, after presenting his case to God that the Almighty has been unjust, Job hears God's response and is brought to the point of recanting his case. But Job does not confess *lament* as a sin against God, for it is not. Rather he comes to recognize the limits of human wisdom before the awesome face of the sovereign Lord..."[1]

God wants us to trust him enough to cry out to him with our laments. Expressing our complaints and grief to the Lord unburdens our souls and enables us to be more receptive to God's counsel. At the same time we also need to trust what Scripture says, that one day God will execute justice in the world.

For the Lord will not forsake his people;
he will not abandon his heritage;
for justice will return to the righteous...
Psalm 94:14-16

The Bible tells us that at his return, Christ will deal justly with sin and evil.[2] All things in our present world that are so wrong will be made right.[3]

Affirm God's Offer

If you or a loved one is near death, a major concern is, "Do I need to fear the judgment of God?" *Judgment* has negative overtones and strikes fear in our hearts.

For we must all appear before
the judgment seat of Christ,
so that each one may receive what
is due for what he has done
in the body, whether good or evil.
2 Corinthians 5:10

After reading 2 Corinthians 5:10 quoted above, we might think we should add up our good deeds to see how they compare with any bad deeds. If the bad outweighs the good, then what? What is the standard by which we are saved from God's wrath against sin?

Our good deeds (what can be seen) are important because they express the faith inside of us (that cannot be seen). But good deeds will never save us because we all have bad deeds (sins). Our bad deeds bring us up short of God's perfect standard for right living.[4] Thank God we do not need to be "perfect" to be saved.

Since no one except Christ can meet God's perfect standard for righteousness, God chooses to transfer the righteousness of Christ to those who have faith in him.

*All have sinned and fall short of the glory of
God, and are justified by his grace as a gift,
through the redemption that is in Christ Jesus,
whom God put forward as a propitiation by his
blood, to be received by faith.*
Romans 3:23-25a

The righteous shall live by faith.
Romans 1:17

If God were to ask you, "Why should I
let you into heaven?" You can answer, "I
believe in Jesus Christ and receive his
righteousness to cover my sin."

This is astounding good news!
Righteousness—being right with God—is a
gift God gives to whoever believes in Jesus
Christ. To be righteous does *not* depend on
how many good deeds we have done. Rather,
to be righteous *depends on Christ's
righteousness* transferred to us by grace
through believing in Christ. Thus, salvation is
not the result of our deeds, but is a gift of
God's grace, his unmerited favor.

By grace you have been saved through faith.
And this is not your own doing; it is the gift of
God, not a result of works…
Ephesians 2:8-9

Does a believer in Jesus Christ need to fear God's judgment? No! At the final judgment, God will judge believers to have received the righteousness of Christ. You will be justified before God—just as if you had never sinned!

There is therefore now no condemnation
for those who are in Christ Jesus….
What then shall we say to these things?
If God is for us, who can be against us?
Romans 8:1,31

What about those who reject the grace of God and refuse to trust in Jesus for rescue from the wrath of God against sin?   Scripture suggests that God will allow them to experience the consequences of their choice, as awful as that may be.[5] None of us is in a position to condemn anyone because only God knows the true heart of a person.[6]

Jesus invites you to open the door of your heart to him.[7] If you have not yet committed yourself to Christ in faith, you can pray now, "Lord, I'm sorry for my sins and I trust Jesus to be my Savior and Lord."

"For God so loved the world, that he gave his only Son, that whoever believes in him should not perish but have eternal life. For God did not send his Son into the world to condemn the world, but in order that the world might be saved through him. Whoever believes in him is not condemned, but whoever does not believe is condemned already, because he has not believed in the name of the only Son of God.
John 3:16-18

My wife, Janiece, experienced a poignant deathbed moment with her mother. When Janiece said to her, "If God were to ask you, 'Why should I let you into heaven?' what would you say?" After a long silence, her mother answered, "Only Jesus." It is a precious memory of her mother's faith in Christ. Can you testify as well to your faith in Jesus?

Scripture makes it clear that there will be a day of judgment when God will set all things right in the world.[8] Bible scholar N.T. Wright comments, "Faced with a world in rebellion, a world full of exploitation and wickedness, a good God must be a God of judgment."[9]

God's judgment is *good news* for the believer. It is because God *loves you and me* that Christ died on the cross to take upon himself the punishment we deserve and redeem us. Let us receive God's good news as the ground receives rain, and be astonished that he showers us with his amazing grace!

I know not why God's wondrous grace
to me he has made known,
nor why, unworthy, Christ in love
redeemed me for his own.
But I know whom I have believed,
and am persuaded the he is able
to keep that which I've committed
unto him against that day.[10]

****

Summary

Since we all must appear before God on the day of judgment, our only hope to be acquitted is that, by God's grace, Christ has paid all the penalty for our sin.

Prayer

Dear Jesus Christ, you are Lord of the universe. You are our coming Judge and Redeemer. I humbly repent of my sin and receive you as my Savior and Lord. Thank you for dying on the cross to pay the penalty I deserve for my sin. Thank you for offering me complete forgiveness now and solid hope for eternity. Amen.

Affirmation

Question: "What is your only comfort, in life and in death?"

Answer: "That I belong—body and soul, in life and in death—not to myself but to my faithful Savior, Jesus Christ, who at the cost of his own blood has fully paid for all my sins and has completely freed me from the dominion of the devil; that he protects me so well that without the will of my Father in heaven not a hair can fall from my head; indeed, that everything must fit his purpose for my salvation. Therefore, by his Holy Spirit, he also assures me of eternal life...."[11]

Help us, O God of our salvation,
for the glory of your name;
deliver us and forgive our sins
for your name's sake!
Psalm 79:9

CHAPTER SIX

What is the Meaning of the "New Heavens and New Earth?"

According to his promise we are waiting for new heavens and a new earth in which righteousness dwells.
2 Peter 3:13

Many people are confused as to what the Bible teaches about the new heavens and new earth. Some commentators have contributed to the confusion by adding wild imagination to what Scripture says. Perhaps at the return of Christ, which inaugurates the new heavens and new earth, everyone will be surprised.

Although details of our eternal existence are a mystery, the Bible does give us a few remarkable descriptions of the promised new creation. Here are three.

1. Earth will be made new.

Can you imagine what the Garden of Eden was like in all of its pristine grandeur? Think of the most beautiful places you have visited. The new earth is expected to be like that, only better. The curse brought by sin will be reversed.

In 2 Peter 3:13 quoted above, Peter teaches that the heavens and earth will be *new*. He echoes the prophet Isaiah who also foretells God's promise:

> *For behold, I create*
> *new heavens and*
> *a new earth....*
> Isaiah 65:17

Do the words *new earth* mean an earth totally different from the earth we know now or do they mean a restoration of the earth? The Greek word for "new" suggests *restoration*. Peter reminds his readers:

God [will] restore *everything, as he promised long ago through his holy prophets.*
Acts 3:21 (NIV)

Restoration suggests *continuity*—connection with the old, the familiar, the well-known, but also a *discontinuity*—forming something new. A good analogy is childbirth.

When a child is born, the child is of course human like the parents. But the child is also fresh, unique; not the same individual as the parents. The new earth will be like that—familiar yet wonderfully new.

What will our eternal existence be like? Ponder this magnificent description in Revelation 21.

Then I saw a new heaven and a new earth, for the first heaven and the first earth had passed away, and there was no longer any sea. I saw the Holy City, the new Jerusalem, coming down out of heaven from God, prepared as a bride beautifully dressed for her husband. And I heard a loud voice from the throne saying, "Look! God's dwelling place is now among the people, and he will dwell with

them. They will be his people, and God himself will be with them and be their God. He will wipe every tear from their eyes. There will be no more death or mourning or crying or pain, for the old order of things has passed away."
Revelation 21:1-4 (NIV)

Imagine these glorious qualities listed in Revelation 21:

- A new heaven and new earth
- No sea (a symbol of evil)
- The holy city (the people of God)
- God himself will dwell with us
- No more tears
- No more death
- No more mourning or crying or pain!

Wow!

2. Heaven and earth will be one.

Heaven is God's "space." In Revelation 21:1-3, we learn that God will make the new earth his dwelling place. Since heaven is where God is, we shall then be in heaven while we are on the new earth.

Bible scholar Anthony Hoekema explains: "Heaven and earth will then no longer be separated, as they are now, but will be one."[1]

Since music and song powerfully express our deepest emotions, we will employ them in the praise of Christ.[2] But the new heavens and earth will be quite different from the popular notion of being somewhere in space wearing white robes and playing harps.

Hoekema explains, "The Bible assures us that God will create a new earth on which we shall live to God's praise in glorified, resurrected bodies. On that new earth, therefore, we hope to spend eternity, enjoying its beauties, exploring its resources, and using its treasures to the glory of God."[3]

3. Righteousness will permeate the new heavens and earth.

The Apostle Peter writes that God has promised us new heavens and a new earth *where righteousness dwells*.[4] That means every believer will be free from sin, free from a me-centered pride, free from prejudice, hate, and injustice.

"Righteousness" does not pervade this earth now. But on the new earth, there will be no need for police or an army. You will not need to lock your home. You will not worry about corruption or serial killers or terrorism.

Righteousness will dwell on the new earth because God dwells there. God's righteousness is just and true. It will permeate every relationship with fullness and completeness. We will not feel alone or misunderstood. We will have perfect communication. Every activity will be inspired by whatever is excellent and commendable. Finally the petition in the Lord's prayer will be fully realized:

> *Your Kingdom come,*
> *Your will be done,*
> *on earth as it is in heaven.*
> Matthew 6:10

Prepare to be surprised by the new heavens and new earth.

No eye has seen, nor ear heard,
nor the heart of man imagined
what God has prepared
for those who love him.
1 Corinthians 2.9

****

Summary

At the return of Christ, heaven and earth will be one, the earth will be newly restored, and righteousness will permeate the new heavens and earth. God will grant us a joy and peace beyond what this earth can offer. The wonder of it all helps us now to look forward to the coming glory.

Prayer

"O God of wonder, God of might,
Grant us some elevated sight,
Of endless days. And let us see
The joy of what is yet to be....

"The blind can see a bird on wing,
The dumb can lift their voice and sing.
The diabetic eats at will,
The coronary runs uphill.

The lame can walk, the deaf can hear,
The cancer ridden bone is clear.
Arthritic joints are lithe and free,
And every pain has ceased to be.
And every sorrow deep within
And every trace of lingering sin
Is gone. And all that's left is joy,
And endless ages to employ
The heart and mind, and understand
And love the sovereign Lord who planned
That it should take eternity
To lavish all his grace on me....

"And guard us by the hope that we,
Through grace on lands you restore,
Are justified for evermore."[5]
(A prayer by John Piper)

CHAPTER SEVEN

WHAT COMFORT DO I HAVE NOW?

And when the chief Shepherd appears,
you will receive the unfading crown of glory.
1 Peter 5:4

Peter says that when Jesus appears at his return, you will receive a crown of glory that will never fade. It will be eternal glory.

You or a loved one might be in a debilitating condition now. Your pain and sadness hang heavy over you like a dark cloud, and it's difficult for you to see any light, any hope. If I were sitting with you, I would listen to your story. Each condition is different; each presents its own challenges. When we had explored adequately how you think and feel now, I would gently suggest we turn to

Scripture and hear what our Wonderful Counselor would offer as comfort.

The Promised Winner's Crown

I think Jesus would comfort us by saying that your reward is coming. When the Apostle Paul reflected on his imminent departure from this life, he wrote:

Now there is in store for me the crown of righteousness, which the Lord, the righteous Judge, will award to me on that day—and not only to me, but also to all who have longed for his appearing.
2 Timothy 4:8

Again Paul uses a sports analogy. "Crown" relates to the Olympic wreath given in ancient times to champions who had endured obstacles and won the contest. The crown consisted of flowers that did not last. Like any achievement in this life, the exhilaration we can get from those wins is limited. But the Apostle Peter reminds us that the victor's crown that Jesus gives to every believer is not temporary; it will not fade.

The "crown of righteousness" refers to the marvelous redeeming righteousness that our Lord Jesus Christ will confer on every believer. If this crown were the result of our own efforts, its value would be temporary. But in fact, this crown was won by Christ's death and resurrection. It's good eternally. This is real comfort that benefits us even now.

The Glory of God

I think Jesus would comfort us by directing our attention to God's glory. As Paul suggests to the Roman Christians, God's glory is inexhaustible. It will take "forever" to explore. We will be eternally grateful for the riches of his grace toward us and his glory in us.

Have you ever wondered what "the glory of God" means? In one sense it includes all God has done in the history of our redemption. Its significance is substantial or *heavy*. Paul talks about the "weight of glory."

So we do not lose heart. Though our outer self is wasting away, our inner self is being

renewed day by day. For this light momentary
affliction is preparing for us
an eternal weight of glory
beyond all comparison....
2 Corinthians 4:17

Wendell Kimbrough put this sense of glory to music:

Oh eternal weight of glory, Oh inheritance
divine, we will see our Lord redeeming every
past and future time. All our pains will be
transfigured like the scars of Christ our Lord,
we will see the weight of glory and our broken
years restored. For behold I tell a mystery:
at the trumpet sound we'll wake!
Every year we thought was wasted,
every night we cried, "How Long?"
All will be a passing moment
in our Savior's victory song.[1]

Glory refers to God being "loaded" with infinite holiness expressed in his grace, power, beauty, goodness, justice, and love. When we glorify God, we honor him for all he is. Each quality is displayed with dazzling brilliance in Jesus Christ.

Long ago, at many times and in many ways,
God spoke to our fathers by the prophets,
but in these last days he has spoken
to us by his Son,
whom he appointed the heir of all things,
through whom also he created the world.
The Son is the radiance of the glory of God...
Hebrews 1:1-3

The radiance of Jesus is reflected in the creation of the world and in the new creation within every believer!

God has chosen to make known...the glorious
riches of this mystery, which is
Christ in you, the hope of glory.
Colossians 1:27

The "hope of glory" is not wishful thought, but a confident, jubilant knowledge in the present that one day we will see Christ face to face.[2]   I find this enormously exciting.

The Encouragement of Scripture

I think Jesus, our Wonderful Counselor, would comfort us now by reminding us of his Word to us. His Word comforted me. When my physical condition grew worse, I was tempted to despair. Then I remembered what some famous theologian had said: "Sometimes you need to beat yourself over the head with Scripture." For this hardheaded Dutchman, I think that is exactly right.

So I searched for Scripture passages that reminded me of God's good news. I read them over and memorized some of them. Following are some verses that renew my mind. As you reflect on them, you too will find your mind *renewed* and, as the Apostle Paul says, you will be *transformed*.[3] You may want to get your mind refreshed now as a helpful preparation for the coming glory celebration.

The Lord is my strength and my song,
and he has become my salvation;
this is my God, and I will praise him...
Exodus 15:2

Be strong and courageous. Do not fear...,
for it is the Lord your God who goes with you.
He will not leave you or forsake you.
Deuteronomy 31:6

I bless the Lord who gives me counsel;
in the night also my heart instructs me.
I have set the Lord always before me;
because he is at my right hand,
I shall not be shaken.
Psalm 16:7-8

I love you, O Lord, my strength.
The Lord is my rock and my fortress and my
deliverer, my God, my rock, in whom I take
refuge, my shield, and the horn of my
salvation, my stronghold.
I call upon the Lord,
who is worthy to be praised...
Psalm 18:1-3

The Lord is my shepherd; I shall not want...
Even though I walk through the valley of the
shadow of death, I will fear no evil,
for you are with me...
Surely goodness and mercy shall follow me
all the days of my life, and I shall dwell in
the house of the Lord forever.
Psalm 23:1,4,6

I trust in you, O Lord;
I say, "You are my God."
My times are in your hand...
Psalm 31:14-15

Precious in the sight of the Lord
is the death of his saints.
Psalm 116:15

Peace I [Jesus] leave with you; my peace I
give to you. Not as the world gives do I give to
you. Let not your hearts be troubled,
neither let them be afraid.
John 14:27

I am sure that neither death nor life,...
nor things present nor things to come,...
nor anything else in all creation,
will be able to separate us from
the love of God in Christ Jesus our Lord.
Romans 8:38-39

I am continually with you;
you hold my right hand.
You guide me with your counsel,
and afterward you will receive me to glory.
Psalm 73:23-24

The time of my departure has come.
I have fought the good fight,
I have finished the race,
I have kept the faith.
Henceforth there is laid up for me
the crown of righteousness,

which the Lord, the righteous judge,
will award to me on that day...
2 Timothy 4:6-8

Behold! I tell you a mystery. We shall not all
sleep, but we shall all be changed, in a
moment, in the twinkling of an eye,
at the last trumpet. For the trumpet will sound,
and the dead will be raised imperishable, and
we shall be changed.... Then shall come to
pass the saying that is written:
"Death is swallowed up in victory."
"O death, where is your victory?
O death, where is your sting?"
The sting of death is sin,
and the power of sin is the law.
But thanks be to God, who gives us
the victory through our Lord Jesus Christ.
1 Corinthians 15:51-52,54-57

Oh, the depth of the riches and wisdom
and knowledge of God! How unsearchable
are his judgments and how inscrutable his
ways!.... For from him and through him
and to him are all things.
To God be glory forever. Amen.
Romans 11:33,36

****

Summary

Dear friends, when the last trumpet sounds and the great Easter bell resounds, "paradise lost" will become "paradise found," and you and I will celebrate the glory of God. Praise the Lord!

Doxology

"Praise God from whom all blessings flow;
praise him, all creatures here below;
praise him above, ye heavenly host;
praise Father, Son, and Holy Ghost. Amen."[4]

ENDNOTES

A NOTE TO THE READER

1. J. Todd Billings, *Rejoicing in Lament: Wrestling with Incurable Cancer & Life in Christ* (Brazos Press, 2015), 33.

Chapter 1: HOW CAN I PREPARE FOR MY DEPARTURE?

1. "The Strife Is O'er, the Battle Done," *Lift Up Your Hearts: Psalms, Hymns, and Spiritual Songs* (Faith Alive,2013), p 185.

2. "For All the Saints," *Lift Up Your Hearts: Psalms, Hymns, and Spiritual Songs* (Faith Alive, 2013), p 254.

Chapter 2: WHAT HAPPENS RIGHT AFTER DEATH?

1. N. T. Wright, *Surprised by Hope: Rethinking Heaven, the Resurrection, and the Mission of the Church* (Harper One, 2008), 171-172.

2. "Going Home," Words by William Arms Fisher and Ken Bible, Music by Antonin Dvorak; arr. by Ken Bible, 2000, by LNWhymns.com. CCLI Song #3636552. (A video depicting images related to the music and lyrics can be seen on YouTube at "Annie Haslam - Going Home").

3. "Precious Lord, Take My Hand," Thomas A. Dorsey, *Lift Up Your Hearts: Psalms, Hymns, and Spiritual Songs* (Faith Alive, 2013), 465.

Chapter 3: HOW CAN I GET READY FOR THE RETURN OF CHRIST?

1. Romans 8:11 *And if the Spirit of him who raised Jesus from the dead is living in you, he who raised Christ from the dead will also give life to your mortal bodies because of his Spirit who lives in you.*

2. Matthew 24:14 *And this gospel of the kingdom will be proclaimed throughout the whole world as a*

testimony to all nations, and then the end will come.

3. Philippians 2:9-11 *Therefore God has highly exalted him and bestowed on him the name that is above every name, so that at the name of Jesus every knee should bow, in heaven and on earth and under the earth, and every tongue confess that Jesus Christ is Lord, to the glory of God the Father.*

4. Matthew 25:31-46 *When the Son of Man comes in his glory, and all the angels with him, then he will sit on his glorious throne. Before him will be gathered all the nations, and he will separate people one from another as a shepherd separates the sheep from the goats. And he will place the sheep on his right, but the goats on the left. Then the King will say to those on his right, "Come, you who are blessed by my Father, inherit the kingdom prepared for you*

from the foundation of the world. For I was hungry and you gave me food, I was thirsty and you gave me drink, I was a stranger and you welcomed me, I was naked and you clothed me, I was sick and you visited me, I was in prison and you came to me." Then the righteous will answer him, saying, "Lord, when did we see you hungry and feed you, or thirsty and give you drink? And when did we see you a stranger and welcome you, or naked and clothe you? And when did we see you sick or in prison and visit you?" And the King will answer them, "Truly, I say to you, as you did it to one of the least of these my brothers, you did it to me." Then he will say to those on his left, "Depart from me, you cursed, into the eternal fire prepared for the devil and his angels. For I was hungry and you gave me no food, I was thirsty and you gave me no drink, I was a stranger and you did not welcome me, naked and you did not clothe me, sick and in prison and you did not visit me." Then they also will answer, saying, "Lord, when did we see you hungry or thirsty or a stranger or naked or sick or in prison, and did not minister to you? Then he will answer them, saying, "Truly, I say to you, as you did not do it to one of the least of these, you did not do it to me." And these will go away into eternal punishment, but the righteous into eternal life.

5. Romans 2:5 *But because of your hard and impenitent heart you are storing up wrath for yourself on the day of wrath when God's righteous judgment will be revealed.*

6. Matthew 25:32-34 *Before him will be gathered all the nations, and he will separate people one from another as a shepherd separates the sheep from the goats. And he will place the*

sheep on his right, but the goats on the left. Then the King will say to those on his right, "Come, you who are blessed by my Father, inherit the kingdom prepared for you from the foundation of the world."

7. 2 Peter 3:13 *But according to his promise we are waiting for new heavens and a new earth in which righteousness dwells.*

8. The Big Bang Theory is a leading scientific explanation about how the universe began. Genesis1:1 says, *In the beginning, God created the heavens and the earth.*

9. Some scientists, such as Professor Brian Cox, predict the end of the universe. In his *Wonders of the Solar System* and *Wonders of the Universe* series, he predicts that everything, including time itself, will cease to exist. Matthew 24:14 states, *And this gospel of the kingdom will be proclaimed throughout the whole*

world as a testimony to all nations, and then the end will come.

10. There are differing views about the sequence of events at the return of Christ. While respecting other biblical interpretations, I take the position that the events related to the return of Christ will occur rather simultaneously.

11. Revelation 1:7 *Behold, he is coming with the clouds, and every eye will see him, even those who pierced him, and all tribes of the earth will wail on account of him. Even so. Amen.*

12. Matthew 24:42-25:30 *Therefore, stay awake, for you do not know on what day your Lord is coming. But know this, that if the master of the house had known in what part of the night the thief was coming, he would have stayed awake and would not have let his house be broken into. Therefore you also must be ready, for the Son of Man is coming at an*

hour you do not expect. Who then is the faithful and wise servant, whom his master has set over his household, to give them their food at the proper time? Blessed is that servant whom his master will find so doing when he comes. Truly, I say to you, he will set him over all his possessions. But if that wicked servant says to himself, "My master is delayed," and begins to beat his fellow servants and eats and drinks with drunkards, the master of that servant will come on a day when he does not expect him and at an hour he does not know and will cut him in pieces and put him with the hypocrites. In that place there will be weeping and gnashing of teeth.

The Parable of the Ten Virgins
Then the kingdom of heaven will be like ten virgins who took their lamps and went to meet the bridegroom. Five of them were foolish, and five were wise.

*For when the foolish took their lamps,
they took no oil with them, but the wise
took flasks of oil with their lamps. As
the bridegroom was delayed, they all
became drowsy and slept. But at
midnight there was a cry, "Here is the
bridegroom! Come out to meet him."
Then all those virgins rose and trimmed
their lamps. And the foolish said to the
wise, "Give us some of your oil, for our
lamps are going out." But the wise
answered, saying, "Since there will not
be enough for us and for you, go rather
to the dealers and buy for yourselves."
And while they were going to buy, the
bridegroom came, and those who were
ready went in with him to the marriage
feast, and the door was shut. Afterward
the other virgins came also, saying,
"Lord, lord, open to us." But he
answered, "Truly, I say to you, I do not
know you." Watch therefore, for you
know neither the day nor the hour.
The Parable of the Talents*

For it will be like a man going on a journey, who called his servants and entrusted to them his property. To one he gave five talents, to another two, to another one, to each according to his ability. Then he went away. He who had received the five talents went at once and traded with them, and he made five talents more. So also he who had the two talents made two talents more. But he who had received the one talent went and dug in the ground and hid his master's money. Now after a long time the master of those servants came and settled accounts with them. And he who had received the five talents came forward, bringing five talents more, saying, "Master, you delivered to me five talents; here, I have made five talents more." His master said to him, "Well done, good and faithful servant. You have been faithful over a little; I will set you over much. Enter into the joy of your master." And he also who had the two talents came forward, saying, "Master, you delivered to me two talents; here, I have made two talents more." His master said to him, "Well done, good and faithful servant. You have been faithful over a little; I will set you over much. Enter into the joy of your master." He also who had received the one talent came forward, saying, "Master, I knew you to be a hard man, reaping where you did not sow, and gathering where you scattered no seed, so I was afraid, and I went and hid your talent in the ground. Here, you have what is yours." But his master answered him, "You wicked and slothful servant! You knew that I reap where I have not sown and gather where I scattered no seed? Then you ought to have invested my money with the bankers, and at my coming I should have received what was my own with interest. So take the talent from him and give it to him who has the ten talents. For to everyone who has will more be given, and he will have an abundance. But from the one who has not, even what he has will be taken away. And cast the worthless servant into the outer darkness. In that place there will be weeping and gnashing of teeth."

13. Matthew 25:1-13 (See endnote #12.)

14. A part of liturgy expressed by many Christians. Most English versions of the Nicene Creed also include the following statements: "...he ascended into heaven and is seated at the right hand of the Father. He will come again in his glory to judge the living and the dead, and his kingdom will have no end. ... We look for the resurrection of the dead, and the life of the world to come."

15. "Eternal Weight of Glory," Wendell Kimbrough, from the album *Psalms We Sing Together,* 2016. wendellk.com

Chapter 4: WHAT WILL THE BODILY RESSURECTION BE LIKE?

1. See Revelation 21:3-4 *And I heard a loud voice from the throne saying, 'Behold, the dwelling place of God is with man. He will dwell with them, and they will be his people, and God himself will be with them as their God. He will wipe away every tear from their eyes, and death shall be no more, neither shall there be mourning, nor crying, nor pain anymore, for the former things have passed away.* Also see Anthony A. Hoekema, *The Bible and The Future* (William B. Eerdmans Publishing Company, 1979) 249.

2. Hoekema, 249.

3. Hoekema, 250.

Chapter 5: HOW CAN I SURVIVE GOD'S JUDGMENT?

1. J. Todd Billings, *Rejoicing in Lament: Wrestling with Incurable Cancer & Life in Christ* (Brazos Press, 2015), 22.

2. Matthew 25:31-32 *When the Son of Man comes in his glory, and all the angels with him, then he will sit on his glorious throne. Before him will be gathered all the nations, and he will separate people one from another as a shepherd separates the sheep from the goats.*

1Corinthians 4:5 *Therefore do not pronounce judgment before the time, before the Lord comes, who will bring to light the things now hidden in darkness and will disclose the purposes of the heart. Then each one will receive his commendation from God.*

Hebrews 9:27-28 *And just as it is appointed for man to die once, and after that comes judgment, so Christ, having been offered once to bear the sins of many, will appear a second time, not to deal with sin but to save those who are eagerly waiting for him.*

3. John 1:29 *The next day he saw Jesus coming toward him, and said, "Behold,*

the Lamb of God, who takes away the
sin of the world!

4. Romans 3:23 *for all have sinned and*
   fall short of the glory of God…

5. John 3:1 *Whoever believes in him is not*
   condemned, but whoever does not
   believe is condemned already, because
   he has not believed in the name of the
   only Son of God.
   Romans 1:18-32 *For the wrath of God*
   is revealed from heaven against all
   ungodliness and unrighteousness of
   men, who by their unrighteousness
   suppress the truth. For what can be
   known about God is plain to them,
   because God has shown it to them. For
   his invisible attributes, namely, his
   eternal power and divine nature, have
   been clearly perceived, ever since the
   creation of the world, in the things that
   have been made. So they are without
   excuse. For although they knew God,
   they did not honor him as God or give
   thanks to him, but they became futile in

their thinking, and their foolish hearts were darkened. Claiming to be wise, they became fools, and exchanged the glory of the immortal God for images resembling mortal man and birds and animals and creeping things.

Therefore God gave them up in the lusts of their hearts to impurity, to the dishonoring of their bodies among themselves, because they exchanged the truth about God for a lie and worshiped and served the creature rather than the Creator, who is blessed forever! Amen. For this reason God gave them up to dishonorable passions. For their women exchanged natural relations for those that are contrary to nature; and the men likewise gave up natural relations with women and were consumed with passion for one another, men committing shameless acts with men and receiving in themselves the due penalty for their error. And since they did not see fit to acknowledge

God, God gave them up to a debased mind to do what ought not to be done. They were filled with all manner of unrighteousness, evil, covetousness, malice. They are full of envy, murder, strife, deceit, maliciousness. They are gossips, slanderers, haters of God, insolent, haughty, boastful, inventors of evil, disobedient to parents, foolish, faithless, heartless, ruthless. Though they know God's righteous decree that those who practice such things deserve to die, they not only do them but give approval to those who practice them.

6. Romans 2:1-4 *Therefore you have no excuse, O man, every one of you who judges. For in passing judgment on another you condemn yourself, because you, the judge, practice the very same things. We know that the judgment of God rightly falls on those who practice such things. Do you suppose, O man— you who judge those who practice such things and yet do them yourself—that*

you will escape the judgment of God? Or do you presume on the riches of his kindness and forbearance and patience, not knowing that God's kindness is meant to lead you to repentance?

7. Revelation 3:20 *Behold, I stand at the door and knock. If anyone hears my voice and opens the door, I will come in to him and eat with him, and he with me.*

8. Acts 17:30-31 *The times of ignorance God overlooked, but now he commands all people everywhere to repent, because he has fixed a day on which he will judge the world in righteousness by a man whom he has appointed; and of this he has given assurance to all by raising him from the dead.*

9. N. T. Wright, *Surprised by Hope: Rethinking Heaven, the Resurrection, and the Mission of the Church* (Harper One, 2008), 137.

10. Daniel W. Whittle, *Lift Up Your Hearts: Psalms, Hymns, and Spiritual Songs* (Faith Alive, 2013), 690.
11. *The Heidelberg Catechism* (United Church Press, 1962), 9.

Chapter 6: WHAT IS THE MEANING OF THE "NEW HEAVENS AND NEW EARTH?"

1. Anthony A. Hoekema, *The Bible and The Future* (William B. Eerdmans Publishing Company, 1979), 274.
2. See for example Revelation 5:9-10.
3. Hoekema, 274.
4. 2 Peter 3:13 *But according to his promise we are waiting for new heavens and a new earth in which righteousness dwells.*
5. "Justified For Evermore" from *Future Grace, Revised Edition: The Purifying Power of the Promises of God* by John Piper, copyright © 1995, 2012 by Desiring God Foundation. WaterBrook Multnomah is an imprint of the Crown Publishing Group, a

Chapter 7: WHAT COMFORT DO I HAVE NOW?

1. "Eternal Weight of Glory" words and music: Wendell Kimbrough, 2016. From the album *Psalms We Sing Together.* wendellk.com

2. 1 Corinthians 13:12 *For now we see in a mirror dimly, but then face to face. Now I know in part; then I shall know fully, even as I have been fully known.*

3. Romans 12:2 *Do not be conformed to this world, but be transformed by the renewing of your mind...*

4. "Praise God from Whom All Blessings Flow," *Lift Up Your Hearts: Psalms, Hymns, and Spiritual Songs* (Faith Alive,2013), 965. You may click on the following link to YouTube to hear the Hope College student body sing an acapella rendition of the Doxology: http://bit.ly/2Ak4isY .

SUMMARIES

Chapter 1: **HOW CAN I PREPARE FOR MY DEPARTURE?**

You can prepare for your departure by affirming your belief in Jesus Christ, who loves you and gives you eternal life.

Chapter 2: **WHAT HAPPENS RIGHT AFTER DEATH?**

Right after death, the soul of the believer is "at home with the Lord;" and that is better than we can imagine.

Chapter 3: **HOW CAN I GET READY FOR THE RETURN OF CHRIST?**

When we set our hope on Jesus, who is our strength and who comforts us in our weakness, we will be ready for the return of Christ.

Chapter 4: **WHAT WILL THE BODILY RESURRECTION BE LIKE?**

The Bible's description of our resurrected bodies is that they will be imperishable, glorious, powerful, spiritual bodies. This gives us hope now knowing that God will give us the final victory over every consequence of sin.

Chapter 5: HOW CAN I FACE GOD'S JUDGMENT?

Since we all must appear before God on the day of judgment, our only hope to be acquitted is that, by God's grace, Christ has paid all the penalty for the believer's sin.

Chapter 6: WHAT IS THE MEANING OF THE "NEW HEAVENS AND NEW EARTH"?

At the return of Christ, heaven and earth will be one, the earth will be newly restored, and righteousness will permeate the new heavens and earth. God will grant us a joy and peace beyond what this earth can offer. The wonder of it all helps us now to look forward to the coming glory.

Chapter 7: WHAT COMFORT DO I HAVE NOW?

Dear friends, when the last trumpet sounds and the great Easter bell resounds, "paradise lost" will become "paradise found," and you and I will celebrate the glory of God. Looking forward to beholding God's glory comforts us now. Praise the Lord!

Let us hold unswervingly to the hope we profess, for he who promised is faithful.
Hebrews 10:23

A FRIEND'S LAMENT

It was graduation day at Trinity Christian College—two years and a month ago—that I took Lois to the emergency room, and she was diagnosed with bile duct cancer. The doctors gave us three months to a year; the Lord gave us 25 months.

We prayed fervently for healing; *you* prayed for healing, and many others— even those we do not know—prayed for healing.

But healing did not come. Three months ago the medical establishment gave up, and Lois entered hospice care at home. For weeks she clung to life, but a week ago Monday she began to decline quickly, and by Thursday morning the cancer had sapped every drop of life from her frail body. The Lord graciously took her gently into his arms.

I am most grateful to all of you for coming this evening to join our family as we remember Lois' life, and lament her death. Thank you for sitting down beside us on our mourning bench.

I did not look forward to Lois' death, nor did she. She and I could take comfort that she would soon be with the Lord, but never could we look forward to her death, not just the moment of death, but the dying.

I must now learn to live without her, but I cannot make peace with Lois' death. There is no peace in death.

Death is awful, death is abnormal, unnatural; death is the mortal enemy of life, not the natural end of a normal life. Indeed, death is demonic.

Cancer is demonic; it slowly eats away at life, and finally kills it.

So I face Lois' death with indignation—not against God, though sometimes I wonder: Why? Why?

Rather, my indignation is against the powers of darkness, against Satan, against evil that causes death.

Our God is a God of life, a God of health, well-being, shalom. God created and meant us to *live*—and thrive in the land of the living.

Death must really hurt him. So as we weep, I'm sure God's tears mingle with ours on this mourning bench.

I face Lois' death with indignation and grief, because:

- Satan inflicted her with a long slow death—for two difficult years with ongoing treatments, multiple complications, and unrelenting aches—until she was so depleted she could not suck liquid up a straw.
- Death has ripped her from the prime of life, at age 56, when she still had so much to contribute, so many songs to play, so many books to read, so much joy to give our family and others.

- Death has robbed her sisters Mary, Ruth, Jane, brother Sylvan, the in-laws, nieces and nephews of a loving and vibrant sibling, aunt, and family member.
- Death has robbed her many friends of a gracious and caring companion.
- Death has robbed the libraries where she worked of a lover of books and patron-friendly librarian.
- The prince of death has robbed the church of a wonderful musician, pianist and organist. She had a feel for playing the soul of a song, the music that lies in the pause between the notes.
- Death has robbed me of the music of my life, my soul-mate, my faithful companion, my lover.
- Death has wrenched from me the intimacy of marriage. Though there were tender moments, for months I could not give her a good hug—it hurt too much. The constant ache inside was so sensitive that touching her body

anywhere was annoying, even a back rub. For months I could not even kiss her on the lips, for fear of spreading some germ that might shorten her life.

- Death has robbed our three children—Heather, Ethan, Lawren—of a tender loving mother. They are in their twenties—too young to lose their mother.

- Death has robbed little Anthony and our future grandkids of a doting grandmother they will never know, or never remember.

So I walk this dark valley with a heavy heart.
I lament her death. It is a time of tears.
But I lament her death with hope.

I look with hope to that day when the Lord will finally vanquish Satan and evil, that day when cancer will be obliterated, that day when pain and tears and death will be no more.

Lois' remains will be buried in the little country cemetery in Alberta where my great-grandparents, my grandparents, my parents, and other family are buried. There she will lie at rest in the shadow of the Almighty, and day after day the breath of the Almighty, the southwest wind, will whistle its gentle tune through the prairie grass that grows above her grave until that wondrous day of her Savior's return.

I look with hope to that day when Lois will be raised—a perfect vibrant body, no more emaciated by cancer—that day when her long, lithe piano fingers, perfectly restored, will once again dance on the keyboard as she accompanies *all of you* in a jubilant dance of praise to our Maker on the New Earth.

Don Sinnema

(Read at the Memorial Service for Lois Sinnema in Evergreen Park, Illinois, June 14, 2006)

FOR FURTHER READING

1. **J. Todd Billings**, *Rejoicing in Lament*, Brazos Press.2015.
Diagnosed with a rare form of incurable cancer at the age of thirty-nine, Christian theologian Todd Billings began grappling with the hard theological questions we face in the midst of crisis: Why me? Why now? Where is God in all of this? Billings moves beyond pat answers toward hope in God's promises.

2. **Timothy Keller**, *The Reason for God*, Dutton, 2008.
Dr. Keller responds to seven common objections to Christianity raised by those searching for true faith.

3. **C.S. Lewis**, *Mere Christianity*, Harper Collins, 1980.
This book has helped me and a multitude of people better understand the basic Christian faith minus cultural

embellishments we tend to add to the faith.

4. **Joni Eareckson Tada**, *When God Weeps*, Zondervan, 1997.
Joni's thirty years in a wheelchair gives her a special understanding of God's connection with suffering and provides a great source of comfort.

5. **Granger Westburg**, *Good Grief*, Fortress Press, 1971, 2011.
For fifty years this classic text has helped millions of readers find comfort and rediscover hope after loss. Good Grief identifies ten stages of grief—shock, emotion, depression, physical distress, panic, guilt, anger, resistance, hope, and acceptance.

ACKNOWLEDGEMENTS

My earliest awareness of biblical teaching on life after death was a sermon by my father, William A. Swets, on the topic, "The King is Coming." I was about five, but have never forgotten the impact it made on me.

During early college years, I seriously questioned some of my foundational beliefs. How could the astounding gospel be true? Through study of God's Word, through living examples of gospel joy, and through reading *Mere Christianity* by C.S. Lewis, God roused me from intellectual slumber and spiritual lethargy.

Later at Hope College in Holland Michigan, I had a professor who taught Greek with a Hungarian accent and delightful humor. Dr. Joseph Ziros told some very sad stories about how the communists invaded the university where he taught, and tortured him. One day he stopped his story and said to the class, "My dear Christian friends, you look like horses…. You have such long faces! Let us live *sub specie aeternitatis*, under the viewpoint of eternity." It became basic to my world-and-life view.

Students, single adults, couples, and seniors at University Reformed Church in Ann Arbor, Michigan, Christ Community Church in Palm Springs, Florida, and Second Presbyterian Church in Memphis, Tennessee, shaped and sharpened my ministry in pastoral care.

Dr. Suzanne McDonald, professor at Western Theological Seminary in Holland Michigan, graciously allowed my wife and me to audit her course on Eschatology, the biblical study of the fulfillment of all God's promises and purposes in the new creation. It provided us a clearer sneak preview into the grand mystery of God's new creation plan.

Dr. Todd Billings, also professor at Western Theological Seminary, helped me reconsider the value of lament both in our discussions and through his excellent book, *Rejoicing in Lament.*

Janiece S.S. Swets, who many years ago courageously agreed to partner with me as my wife, has daily offered me her love, wisdom, and ruthless editing competence…with humor and joy. I love her.

What incredible blessings from God these and so many others have had on my life. I'm profoundly grateful. To God be all glory!

To God Be The Glory

"Great things he has taught us,
Great things he has done,
And great our rejoicing through Jesus the Son;
But purer and higher and greater will be
Our wonder, our transport,
When Jesus we see."
Fanny J Crosby

ABOUT THE AUTHOR

I learned caring ministry first from my father, William A. Swets, long before he served as Minister of Pastoral Care at Coral Ridge Presbyterian Church in Fort Lauderdale, Florida. Along with my mother, he parented me and my five sisters with firmness and caring.

At Hope College in Holland, Michigan, I majored in Psychology because I wanted to know why we behave as we do. I wanted to know and positively influence behavior through the gifts, training, and circumstances I had been given.

During my junior year at Hope, I asked myself how I could best use any gift granted to me. I came to believe that helping people to know God was the most important task for me, and felt God was leading me to prepare for ministry at Western Theological Seminary in Holland, Michigan.

After serving as a campus minister at the University of Michigan, and senior minister of a small church in Florida, I was called to be Minister of Pastoral Care at Second Presbyterian Church in Memphis, Tennessee.

The "time for my departure" is getting closer day by day. Although I deeply love this life, I can hardly wait for the coming glory.

Contact

You are welcome to contact me at dr.swets@gmail.com.

For further information, go to http://www.findinghappiness.info.

To purchase multiple copies of *The Coming Glory*, contact me or go to http://amzn.to/2CpXxWS.